D1613592

EXPLORING COUNTRIES

Colombia

by Walter Simmons

BELLWETHER MEDIA · MINNEAPOLIS, MN

Note to Librarians, Teachers, and Parents:

Blastoff! Readers are carefully developed by literacy experts and combine standards-based content with developmentally appropriate text.

Level 1 provides the most support through repetition of high-frequency words, light text, predictable sentence patterns, and strong visual support.

Level 2 offers early readers a bit more challenge through varied simple sentences, increased text load, and less repetition of high-frequency words.

Level 3 advances early-fluent readers toward fluency through increased text and concept load, less reliance on visuals, longer sentences, and more literary language.

Level 4 builds reading stamina by providing more text per page, increased use of punctuation, greater variation in sentence patterns, and increasingly challenging vocabulary.

Level 5 encourages children to move from "learning to read" to "reading to learn" by providing even more text, varied writing styles, and less familiar topics.

Whichever book is right for your reader, Blastoff! Readers are the perfect books to build confidence and encourage a love of reading that will last a lifetime!

This edition first published in 2012 by Bellwether Media, Inc.

No part of this publication may be reproduced in whole or in part without written permission of the publisher. For information regarding permission, write to Bellwether Media, Inc., Attention: Permissions Department, 5357 Penn Avenue South, Minneapolis, MN 55419.

Library of Congress Cataloging-in-Publication Data
Simmons, Walter (Walter G.)
  Colombia / by Walter Simmons.
    p. cm. – (Blastoff! readers. Exploring countries)
  Includes bibliographical references and index.
  Summary: "Developed by literacy experts for students in grades three through seven, this book introduces young readers to the geography and culture of Colombia"–Provided by publisher.
  ISBN 978-1-60014-727-2 (hardcover : alk. paper)
  1. Colombia–Juvenile literature. I. Title.
  F2258.5.S56 2012
  986.1–dc23   2011029472

Printed in the United States of America, North Mankato, MN.
010112   1203

Contents

Where Is Colombia?

Caribbean
Sea

Panama

Venezuela

Pacific
Ocean

Colombia

N

W   E

S

★ Bogotá

Did you know?

Colombia was named after explorer
Christopher Columbus. During his
travels, he visited the northern coasts
of South America.

Ecuador

Peru

Colombia is a country in the northwestern corner of South America. It covers 439,736 square miles (1,138,910 square kilometers). Bogotá is its capital and largest city, with more than 8 million people.

Colombia borders Venezuela to the east and Brazil to the southeast. Peru lies to the south, and Ecuador to the southwest. Colombia's western seacoast meets the Pacific Ocean. The Caribbean Sea touches Colombia in the north, where Colombia also shares a short border with Panama.

Brazil

fun fact

Bogotá is one of the highest capital cities in the world. It sits at 8,660 feet (2,640 meters) above sea level. Only the capitals of Bolivia and Ecuador are higher.

Andes Mountains

Mountains, plains, and rain forests cover the Colombian landscape. The Magdalena and Cauca rivers flow north through the Andes Mountains. They divide the Andes into the Cordilleras Occidental, Central, and Oriental. Colombia reaches its highest point at the twin peaks of Christopher Columbus and Simón Bolívar. These snowcapped mountains rise to a height of 18,947 feet (5,775 meters) in the Sierra Nevada de Santa Marta range.

In eastern Colombia is the Llanos. A grassy **savannah** covers the flat plains of this region. The Orinoco and other rivers run east, and several **tributaries** flow south to the Amazon River. The Amazon Rain Forest, the largest tropical forest in the world, fills the southeast.

Orinoco River

To the west of the Andes is the Chocó. This is a rainy jungle region that slopes down to the Pacific Ocean. The Chocó stretches north into the Darién. The Darién region covers the border between Panama and Colombia. There are no roads across the Darién Gap, where a dense rain forest grows.

In the Chocó, small towns hug the seacoast, and scattered villages lie in the mountains. Many of the people belong to the Emberá group of **Amerindians**. They hunt and fish to survive. Other people in the Chocó descend from African slaves who came to Colombia when it was a Spanish **colony**. The mountains and forests isolate those in the Chocó from the rest of Colombia.

fun fact

Lloró, a town in the Chocó, is the rainiest place on Earth. The average rainfall there is more than 500 inches (1,270 centimeters) every year.

howler
monkey

Andean condor

giant
earthworm

fun fact
Colombia has giant
earthworms that grow
6 feet (1.8 meters) long!

Wildlife thrives in the Colombian countryside. Pumas and jaguars prowl the mountains and the rain forests. They share the land with giant armadillos, howler monkeys, and the capybara, a huge jungle rat. The spectacled bear is the only bear **species** that lives in Colombia.

poison dart frog

Did you know?
One of the most dangerous animals in Colombia is the poison dart frog. This brightly colored frog oozes deadly poison from its skin. People in the Chocó use the poison on their hunting darts and arrows.

Colombia is also home to thousands of butterfly species. They share the sky with harpy eagles and Andean condors. The condor is Colombia's national bird. In the lowlands, caimans hunt in the fast streams. Whales, dolphins, and sharks swim in the coastal waters.

More than 45 million people live in Colombia. About three out of every five Colombians are *mestizos*. They have a mixed family background, with European and Amerindian **ancestors**. *Criollos* are people with Spanish ancestors. About one Colombian out of every five is *Criollo*. They speak Spanish, the country's official language.

Amerindians have lived in Colombia for thousands of years. Over the centuries, many tribes have disappeared. Some Amerindians married European or African newcomers. The few remaining Amerindian groups live in the Amazon Rain Forest and the Chocó.

Speak Spanish!

English	Spanish	How to say it
hello	hola	OH-lah
good-bye	adios	ah-dee-OHS
yes	sí	SEE
no	no	NOH
please	por favor	POHR fah-VOR
thank you	gracias	GRAH-see-uhs
friend (male)	amigo	ah-MEE-goh
friend (female)	amiga	ah-MEE-gah

About three out of every four Colombians live in cities. The cities are made up of large *barrios*, or neighborhoods. Each *barrio* has both a shopping and **residential district**. At night, many people go out to visit friends. They gather in streets and **plazas**, eat at restaurants, and go shopping.

Public buses link the cities to the countryside. Small towns serve as market centers for nearby farmers. Farmers in Colombia rise early to work their fields. They **till** the soil and plant in the spring. In the fall, they bring the harvest to nearby towns to sell.

Where People Live in Colombia

countryside
25%

cities
75%

Did you know?
Family is very important in Colombia. Protecting one's *abolengo*, or family name and pride, is a priority.

In Colombia, the school year usually lasts from February until November, with a break in June. Kids must attend school for at least five years. They start school at age 6 or 7. Elementary school focuses on reading, spelling, geography, and math.

After elementary school, students may continue to middle school for grades six to nine. High school includes grades ten and eleven. At this level, students can train for a job or prepare for university studies. If they complete high school, they earn a *bachillerato* degree. They must pass a difficult test to enter a university.

Did you know?

Some schools in Colombia are so crowded that the classrooms work in shifts. Some students come in the morning, and some in the afternoon.

Did you know?

In remote mountain streams, Colombian miners search for rare emeralds. Colombia is one of the world's leading producers of these green gemstones.

Where People Work in Colombia

manufacturing 13%

services 69%

farming 18%

Most Colombian workers have **service jobs**.
They work for banks, airlines, and other businesses
that provide important services. Other Colombians
work in factories, making cement, food products,
chemicals, clothing, and steel.

Many farmers in Colombia grow coffee beans.
The country has more than 500,000 coffee farms.
Colombian farmers also grow corn, bananas,
sugarcane, and cocoa beans. Flowers are
another important farm product. Colombia
exports millions of flowers to the United
States and other countries every year.

The most popular sport in Colombia is soccer.
The national team often competes in the **World Cup**.
Colombians also enjoy professional cycling, baseball,
and bullfighting. In a bullfight, a *matador* uses his skill
and speed to dodge a dangerous bull.

Colombians also enjoy many other activities. Video games are popular in homes and at Internet cafés. The game of *tejo* is another favorite. In *tejo*, a metal disk is thrown at a small box in a sand pit. The box contains **gunpowder**. If the disk hits the middle of the box, boom! The player that earns the most points wins the game.

fun fact

Tejo was played over 500 years ago by peoples native to Colombia.

tejo

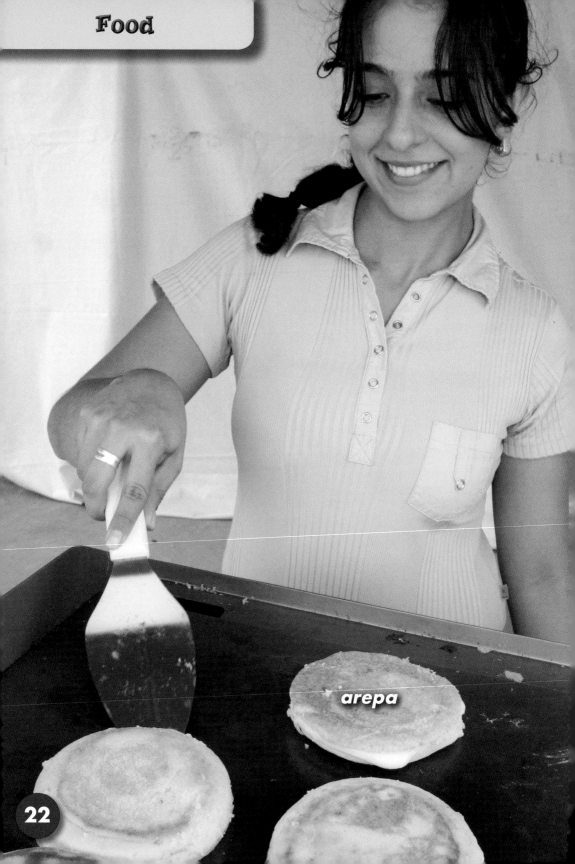

arepa

22

Colombians have an early breakfast, a midday meal, and a late dinner. In the morning, they may enjoy strong coffee, bread, and *changua*. This is a hot soup made with milk, eggs, **cilantro**, and **scallions**.

The midday lunch often includes *empanadas*, which are small pastries filled with meat and vegetables. Fried **plantains** appear along with **yucca** and *arepa*, a bread made from cornmeal. Colombians enjoy fruit juices all day long, especially when it is hot outside.

Many dinners include *ajiaco*, a soup made by boiling chicken, corn, and potatoes. To make *tamales*, cooks fill dough with vegetables and either beef or chicken. They wrap the mixture in a plantain leaf and steam it. Popular desserts are rice pudding and *dulce de leche*, a pudding made with cinnamon, milk, and sugar.

empanadas

ajiaco

fun fact

During *Carnival*, the city of Barranquilla throws a noisy party that lasts four days. Traffic comes to a stop as bands play and thousands of people dance in the streets.

Independence Day

Most Colombians celebrate **Catholic** holidays. The Christmas season begins on December 7 and includes family parties and gift giving. *Carnival* occurs several weeks before Easter. During this holiday, parades and celebrations fill the streets. On Easter Sunday, churches hold a special **procession** through the city.

Independence Day falls on July 20. On this day, Colombians celebrate their independence from Spain. August 7 marks the victory of Simón Bolívar at the Battle of Boyacá. This event helped Colombia end its history as a Spanish colony. Flags and banners decorate the cities, and many towns hold parades.

The Coffee Triangle

Colombia produces some of the world's best coffee. About half of all the nation's coffee comes from an area known as the Coffee Triangle. This region includes Caldas, Quindío, and Risaralda.

fun fact

Many Colombian coffee growers use Jeeps to get around their hilly farms. The town of Armenia celebrates the Jeep every year with a *Yipao*, or Jeep parade. Owners decorate their Jeeps and pile them high with food, furniture, and other goods.

Thousands of small coffee farms spread across the hills. The Colombian National Coffee Park is also in the triangle. It features a coffee museum and an amusement park. The Coffee Triangle draws visitors from around the world and produces coffee that makes Colombia famous.

Fast Facts About Colombia

Colombia's Flag

The flag of Colombia shows three horizontal bands of color. The top half is yellow, and the bottom half is blue and red. Yellow stands for Colombia's gold, while blue stands for the sea. The color red symbolizes the blood shed in the nation's wars for independence. Colombia adopted the flag in 1861.

Official Name: Republic of Colombia

Area: 439,736 square miles (1,138,910 square kilometers); Colombia is the 26th largest country in the world.

Capital City:	Bogotá
Important Cities:	Cali, Medellín, Barranquilla, Cartagena
Population:	44,725,543 (July 2011)
Official Language:	Spanish
National Holiday:	Independence Day (July 20)
Religions:	Christian (90%), Other (10%)
Major Industries:	farming, fishing, manufacturing, mining, services
Natural Resources:	coal, natural gas, iron ore, nickel, copper, emeralds, gold, platinum
Manufactured Products:	textiles, food products, beverages, steel, chemicals, tires, shoes
Farm Products:	coffee beans, bananas, sugarcane, cocoa beans, flowers, rice, plantains
Unit of Money:	Colombian peso; the peso is divided into 100 centavos.

Glossary

Amerindians—peoples originally from North, South, or Central America

ancestors—family members who lived long ago

Catholic—related to the Roman Catholic Church; Roman Catholics are Christian.

cilantro—a leafy herb used in many Colombian dishes

colony—a territory owned and settled by people from another country

exports—sells and sends to another country

gunpowder—an explosive mixture of chemicals or substances

plantains—tropical fruits that look like bananas; Colombian cooks often fry plantains.

plazas—large open spaces in cities or towns where people gather and shop

procession—a crowd of people that moves in an orderly, respectful manner; processions are held in honor of important people or events.

residential district—an area of a city that contains mostly homes and apartments

savannah—a dry grassland habitat

scallions—long green onions that are often used in Colombian cooking

service jobs—jobs that perform tasks for people or businesses

species—specific kinds of living things; members of a species share the same characteristics.

till—to dig up soil and prepare it for planting

tributaries—streams or rivers that flow into larger streams or rivers

World Cup—an international soccer competition held every four years

yucca—a thick root that Colombian cooks fry or boil and serve as a side dish

To Learn More

AT THE LIBRARY

Croy, Anita. *Colombia*. Washington, D.C.: National Geographic, 2008.

Gelletly, LeeAnne. *Colombia*. Broomall, Pa.: Mason Crest Publishers, 2009.

Morrison, Marion. *Colombia*. New York, N.Y.: Children's Press/Scholastic, 2008.

ON THE WEB

Learning more about Colombia is as easy as 1, 2, 3.

1. Go to www.factsurfer.com.

2. Enter "Colombia" into the search box.

3. Click the "Surf" button and you will see a list of related Web sites.

With factsurfer.com, finding more information is just a click away.

Index